BEHIND THE SCREENS

THROUGH THE EYES OF "THE EDWARDS EMPIRE"

WRITTEN BY: IVAN EDWARDS

Copyright © 2024

All Rights Reserved

Publisher: The Mason Publishing Company

This Book contains privacy of the author you cannot copy or duplicate this book all rights reserved. No part of this publication may be reproduced, stored in a retrieval system, or transmitted in any form or by any means -electronic, mechanical, photocopy, recording, or any other- except for brief quotations in printed reviews, without the prior permission of the publisher. For information address Themasonpublishingcompany@gmail.com

printed in the United States of America

ISBN: 979-8-218-97187-8

Table Of Contents

Title Page

Copyright Page...1

Table of Contents..2

Acknowledgements...4

Dedication..5

Introduction...6

Chapter 1 "5...4...3...2...1"..8

Chapter 2 "Start The Live" 12

Chapter 3 Resume Live Broadcast..................................15

Chapter 4 Resume Live Broadcast..................................23

Chapter 5 Resume Live Broadcast..................................28

Chapter 6 Resume Live Broadcast in Arkansas................35

Chapter 7 Wedding Bells..40

Chapter 8 The Family life...42

Chapter 9 Foursome..47

Chapter 10 Girlfriend...51

Chapter 11 Studsband..56

Chapter 12 What about me?..61

Chapter 13 Who's Next?..65

Chapter 14 She likes what she like.............................69

Chapter 15 Club Chic...73

Chapter 16 She's our girl now.....................................80

Chapter 17 Toxic..87

Chapter 18 Fugitive...95

Chapter 19 Drama...99

Chapter 20 Mixed Emotions.....................................109

Chapter 21 Bye Cali..117

Chapter 22 Texas...121

Chapter 23 The Daughter Ex....................................129

Chapter 24 Surgery...139

Chapter 25 It's finally over.......................................145

Chapter 26 She's a fling..154

Chapter 27 The last live..157

Chapter 28 New Life...173

Chapter 29 False Identity..182

Chapter 30 What Baby?..192

Declaration..197

Acknowledgements

I acknowledge God who is the head of my life and blessing me daily allowing me to breathe and be able to do all things possible according to his riches and glory 1.8oz baby very thankful for my life.

Dedication

I dedicate it to my fan's followers and supporters over these 10 years who have seen and heard everything but never seen anything and if nobody believes me ask me and ask around.

Introduction

This is just a book to let everyone know about my life behind the screens of Facebook lives what was really happening vs what was happening only for the lives and awareness basically not to let no one take control of your life.

Some of the characters' names in this book are changed to respect and protect their privacy.

But....

IF YOU KNOW YOU KNOW!

Chapter 1

"5...4...3...2...1"

What's the deal how you feel, here's a little something you didn't know here's how it all started let's go I mean I wasn't that bad. "If you think you can do better than you take him!" Said my mother, scorned and tired from the daily troubles I was introducing to my families' lives. Turning to me, April says, "Alright, well get your stuff." So, I packed my things. I really left my mother's home; April really took me with her, At the age of 13 I was moving in with a 23-year-old woman, her baby daddy, and her kids.

1 WEEK PRIOR

"Come on bro," my brother Walker yelled from the door, "I'm heading out to the party. Are you coming?" I ran to the door to meet him. We headed out to attend my older brother's girlfriend, Nessa's, party. I was eager to attend because Nessa's younger siblings were my friends. Her little brothers name was Christian. Christian, his sister, twin cousins, and I attended the same jr high school. I also hung out with Christian's twin cousins who lived next door. They all were going to be there; Christian was a wrestler at the school. I had attended one of his matches and was introduced to his uncles' baby mother and his step-aunt, April, afterwards, he lived with them. During the party April's eye was on me all night, she looked over at me and that's when I heard a voice say, "Are you going to battle anyone." I looked up to April talking to me about battling with someone on the dance floor. I quickly responded "No" and I said it timidly while remaining in my chair. I sat and watched the wrestling match until I got ready to leave. April gave Walker and I a ride home and invited us to another party she was having for her one-year-old child. When we got to my mother's house April walked with us to the door. I opened the door being greeted by my mother who had not too long came in herself. April introduces herself and they begin to have a dialogue about my behavior. My mother expressed her anger at my choices and how tired she was becoming of me. April looks at me then back to my mom. "Oh, he can't be that bad," by the end of the conversation, I had packed my stuff and got back in the car with April. I was now moving in with my best friend's aunt and family. In the mind of a 13-year-old all I was thinking about was being closer to my friends. I just knew I had just got the best offer given to me. I was free! NO PARENTS, closer to my friends, and no boundaries. I had just signed a deal with the devil that would last for the next, almost, 18 years of my life.

Chapter 2

"Start The Live..."

Growing up I stayed in trouble, so I always understood my mothers' decision in me being placed with April to begin with. Thinking back on the past I wish she would've never allowed or even jokingly made a statement like that. If she knew what all was being done in the hands of another grown woman there wouldn't be no "Edwards Empire" as of today. Initially, living with April was a normal adult child situation. April took me to and from school in the van on most days. If I wanted to leave early I did just that with one call, I thought I was the man at 13. I had it made not only in my mind, but my friends also thought I did. One day I got in trouble at school, and I vividly remember April coming to pick me up early. I remember her saying "Now how you going to be my little boyfriend and you keep getting in trouble?" That was the first time I noticed that there might be something more to April than I was thinking.

April's step nephew Christian lived with her and his uncle, Christian's uncle put fear in his heart. He was a 6'7" big broad man who didn't mind putting his hands on him. They called him uncle Jello, and Uncle Jello was April's current boyfriend and youngest child's father. Christian had an infatuation with his step aunt. He used to stay up at night knowing April was going to be walking round the house naked. The day he told me about it that's when I wanted to find out was it true, she came out the room in a freakin' jersey and it blew Christian smile right off of his face. He banged his head on the pillow repeatedly until he fell asleep. The next morning, we had school, when we got to school, I asked Christian why he had been so quiet and why did he lie about his aunt the night before, "are you kidding me," said Christian, "she had on clothes because you're in the house now." I shrugged it off and went to class that day thinking about what the view was like under that jersey.

Chapter 3

Resume Live Broadcast

After so long April began undoubtedly showing her interest of lust in me. Her body language had begun changing when her child's father would leave, that's when she started pulling her pants down and showing me her ass, she even would allow me to "dry hump" her from behind in places such as the garage. Nobody in the house suspected anything besides Christian. We would have multiple random flirtatious moments in the beginning of me moving in with her. Eventually her baby daddy started to wonder because we would always go for rides and find reasons to leave together. It was even a difference in punishments between Christian and I. Our punishments were even different I started not getting in trouble for things while Christian did. Uncle Jello would argue with April for me to leave and she would tell him I had nowhere to go, that way it will get him to allow me to stay. During this time, I was in a continuation school, a continuation school is a school to help students get caught up that fall behind on credits and it helps put them in their correct grade. That wasn't my issue, see me I completed and skipped past the 8th grade. I went from the 7th to 9th. Christian started to get jealous, and all the cousins also began to start noticing what was going on between April and I. Time began running short because now my mother wanted me to come back home. I had been living my life almost as an adult and wasn't trying to go back under my mother's roof, but I did, I had no choice. I'm now back at home and my mom enrolls me back into a public school. That stay with April did nothing for me but made me think I was grown for real. I had my way there and wasn't switching it up no matter who didn't like it. I started high school with my 2 older siblings.

After a few weeks gone by while living with my mom, I had been introduced to my sister's friend's cousin named TT, that day TT was giving us a ride to school. After we got there everyone jumped out of the car to go their own way and TT tells me to wait. "Okay" I said questioning what was going on, "I want to have relations with you." TT said looking me in my eyes.

"Whhhaaaaaaatttttt, who me? ok" I said excitedly. Young bull was finally about to see what the talk was about. I was "grown" at the age of 14 and was tired of dry humping, besides I couldn't wait to brag to my friends about really having sex. That day I went to school singing "SEX ME BABY, BABY, SEX MEEEEEEEE". I had TT on my mind heavy but didn't want to overhype the situation just in case it really didn't happen. The last bell rang for the day of being release from school. I walked across the street to go to the store and go about my way. I look up and see TT standing on the other side of the street. TT walked up to me with a bag claiming she had a gift for me, I opened the bag, and it was a shirt with rhinestones on it. The same as I wore today, I said thank you and we left together to go to my mother's house who I knew wasn't home. The whole ride I'm singing "I aint never did this before. NOO!" in my J. Cole voice. We get to my moms, and I immediately needed to calm my nerves and with a straight face, like a TRUE LIBRA, I asked, "you tryin to smoke?" She nodded her head yes, so; I went to get a bag of dro to smoke. We smoked, and talked for a little while, then next thing you know I'm lying on the bathroom floor while this 23-year-old woman was having her way with me. TT did what April hadn't done yet, and that was going "ALL THE WAY" with me. At that time, I was sharing a room with my older brother and didn't want to get caught so she decided we go in the bathroom. She used her mouth and aroused me! This was my first real flesh on flesh experience. TT laid me flat on my back, she sat on top of my privates and began to ride me. At that moment I had lost my virginity and became her boyfriend that day.

A week goes by and I'm starting to feel myself, walker and I had been butting heads badly at this point. Looking back on it I did not want to be controlled by anyone. I was put in so many positions to be a man I felt no one could tell me anything. On this day the beef between my older brother and I had got so intense we physically fought. I was so angry at the situation I tried leaving and he wouldn't let me. That day I packed my bags and became a runaway. I had a plan in motion to catch a ride with my new adult girlfriend to Los Angeles. I went to my friend's house, and I called TT to come get me, I chilled until I was picked up. L.A. was an hour and a half away, but I had lucked up because TT was already going that way, she was probably going to be with her real boyfriend, somebody closer in age, but I didn't care. I just wanted a ride away from home, the whole ride was pretty much just music playing. TT really didn't have much to say to me and same with me to her. I had a lot on my mind and was still angry at the situation with my brother. We made it to LA, and she dropped me off at my granny's house at around 12:30 AM. I said my

goodbye, went inside and I laid down and went to sleep.

Chapter 4

Resume Live Broadcast

I woke up in LA at my granny's house, I overheard her on the phone with whom I now know to have been my mother. "Well, do what you gotta do, I guess." says granny.

There was a knock on the door and approximately 10 minutes after that phone call I was in handcuffs, my mother had reported me as a juvenile runaway and now I was in the back of a cop car. I was surprised not to be taken back to my mother's house but instead to juvenile hall. I spent the night there and I couldn't believe it. The next morning, I called my mom hoping she was going to tell them to release me back to her, but she didn't, she told the damn police to keep me. The only other number I knew was my aunt, thankfully she answered and had her senses to agree to pick me up, she only lived 10 minutes away and I was so relieved.

Now here I am living with my aunt, she enrolled me in school, gave me some clothes from my cousins, and took me to the store to buy me some minutes for my boost mobile "chirp phone. We go back to her house and I'm just there chilling with my cousin. I hadn't put the minutes on my phone yet, so I remembered to do that. As soon as I added the minutes on the phone the notifications went off. It was a message from April. I guess my mother had called her looking for me after the situation with my brother. I responded to April's message telling her I was in LA at my aunts, and she asked if I wanted her to pick me up because my friend "(Christian)" missed me and wanted to hang out with me. I said, "I have to be back in the morning." I was supposed to start school the next day and it was already 10:30pm at night, but I didn't care. They came and picked me up, and we drove back up the hill. I sat in the front with April and Christian was in the back. We listened to music during the ride. While driving, April put a gummy worm in her mouth and told me to bite the other side, then we kissed. Christian watched and yelled "Ooooh, I heard that, yall kissed" and he was so mad. Mind you Christian was obsessed with April at this time, he didn't speak for the rest of the ride. We finally made it up the hill, she took me to her new house, and showed me around. I went in the backyard and smoked a blunt. Christian hit it and immediately got goofy as hell, the blunt had knocked him out. April sees Christian had fallen asleep, so she showed me the bedroom, after she showed me the bedroom I went to the room, I laid in the bed and went to sleep. Christian had helped April move in so the next morning she took him back to her baby daddy Jellos house. April goes inside to pick up something and finds Jello in the bed with another man or woman something like that, but it made her mad to where she stormed out of the house. The ride back to her house she's letting out her frustrations to me. We walk back into Aprils and start doing a little work in the home. We began rearranging furniture and unloading boxes until April pulled her pants down, she went into the room, got on the bed and began arching her back and poking her butt out. We had intercourse, and before you know it, I found myself moving in with April. I called my aunt and told her I'm not coming back. I enrolled into high school close to April's house, I went to school when I was pleased and was picked up by April, on demand. I was back in my comfort zone in what I thought in my mind, was a "MAN."

Chapter 5

Resume Live Broadcast

I continued with school until I just didn't want too anymore. April continued doing adult things with me, I was around 16 at this time and I thought things were going great until Jello popped back up and begged to be back in her life. I don't know if she couldn't tell him no or did tell him no, but he found his way back in. Next thing you know I had to go back to playing the kid. Jello had taken back his spot in the bed and I was now in a room alone. I started going back to school and started making friends, by friends I meant home girls who would call the house for me daily. April would be infuriated at the fact other females was talking to me, but she had to play along.

I remember times we would go out as a "family", and I would feel so awkward thinking about all the things April and I had done together. Everyone always thought Jello was my uncle I guess because I was a black boy living with a biracial couple. Now people look at me thinking "how could you go from living with your uncle to taking your uncles wife." Now the truth is out I was only friends with his nephew while is wife was grooming me to be the man, he wasn't to her." This time around a wedding came in plan. April and Jello were getting married, I was asked to be the best man. Christian was also in the wedding along with my little sister, better known on the screen as "Shut up Mookie", so now they were officially together again. I still stayed in the home with them but not Christian. Everything was going well until one day we were all about to leave and I couldn't find the keys. I told April I couldn't find the keys, Jello walks over to me and pushes me on the ground and says, "find the keys nigga!" We were upstairs when he did this, and he almost had me fall off a banister. That was enough for me, I packed up and left Aprils and went to my mother's new house. My mom had moved into a house closer to my stepdads, I would find myself going back and forth between the two houses as I pleased. I was now 17 and had a car, I would drive around all day with no license. Eventually one day, after leaving Aprils side of town, I went through a checkpoint, and the police took my car. Luckily April was behind me because we had just got into an argument, and she was following me because I drove away angry. April gave me a ride to my mom's house. The next couple of days April was in front of my mom's telling us about how her marriage isn't working and she's about to get a divorce, I told her that was crazy. The marriage lasted briefly; I don't know fully why their marriage didn't last; I think Jello was still attracted to men. Meantime I was still currently going to school, ever since I had lost my car, I didn't have a way back and forth from school to my mom's. So, guess who offered to take me to and from school, yep! You guessed it, "April"! We weren't doing sexual acts at this time, but her marriage was failing. Once April finally got a divorce, she moved 3 minutes away from my mom's new house. Of course, I'm 17 now I am as grown as I thought I was at 13. I was living free, had money, a car, and tattoos, she comes back around telling me how close she moved to where I was staying with my mom and persuades me to come back to stay with her. What do you think I did? Yeah, I moved back in with the woman, and I enrolled into another school that was closer to us now. I went there for a few months.

One day my cousin and I ended up chilling and he asked me to give him a Lil Wayne CD and I wanted to know why, he stated that because he was going out that night, I told him he should just chill and stay with us.

My cousin was affiliated with the streets, and I just wanted him to be safe, he ended up going out anyways. That night I found myself with the police pointing guns over the fence while I was in the backyard smoking. I was taken into the house and the police began telling us who they were looking for, we immediately denied knowing the name they called, not knowing it was an alias for my cousin. My mother begins telling the police who everyone in the house was, she started introducing her girlfriend, then me, then April as "my sons' girlfriend", and telling them we live down the street. This was a major mistake not only was I a minor, but April was also a 30-year-old woman. April and I had never really made anything official though. The police made us go to our house and they began searching for it. That night ended with my cousin and I both in the same jail. After 10 hours of being there I saw my cousin and an hour later they uncuffed me and I was released. To this day I still don't know why I was there. When I was released, I went outside just to see April standing right there. I guess since it was suggested that she was my girl and I was her man, I found myself labeled as April's boyfriend let my mom tell it, now at this point we were officially a couple.

Chapter 6

Resume Live In Arkansas

After that incident April began to question being in Cali, she was originally from Arkansas and that's where her family was. One day we had a conversation and April suggested that we go back to Arkansas because of all the troubles occurring in California, I didn't mind. I really had an "I don't give a F***" mentality. At this time, I was 18 and we could be on the record as a couple and move freely. I was now considered legal, my brother Walker was not dating Nessa anymore, but he moved on to her little sister, "NayNay". See NayNay was also Christian's sister. Christian was Jello's nephew that lived with us.

Jello was April's baby daddy, whewwww, did I lose you? So basically, she was April's step niece, you can say NayNay was the favorite out of them all. One day it was me, April, her kids, her sister Flower, along with my brother Walker and NayNay, we all hit the road and we moved to Arkansas to start fresh. As we got off the freeway and made it into Arkansas we went to her grandparents' house, we had planned to stay on the property they said that they had, it was a house they owned, when we got there, we were welcomed to a one-bedroom trailer home that we made work and showed gratitude for. We stayed in the house for a while but also looked for places to move. During this time April began to rekindle relationships with her grandmother and siblings but we had to get out of there.

We finally found an apartment complex with two apartments right across from each other. Walker and NayNay moved in one and our family in the other. Eventually Walker ended up leaving and going back to California a few months later, so did NayNay. We struggled hard for a while, we often went to food banks to get expired can goods and cold pizzas. Our car ended up getting repossessed because we couldn't afford the payments, the sad thing was it was only one payment left that was owed on our car. Luckily, I was working at Wal-Mart and was able to get another car the same day. Eventually April started working at Wal-Mart as well.

She worked at a different location than me. We needed another car to accommodate us and to make sure we both got back and forth to work. I worked overnight and she worked all day. April ended up going to the same car lot as me and found her a car. Things were coming along and looking up for us.

1 year later, Ring! Ring!

"Hey Nephew, I need you to come home so you can get this money" says Auntie in California, that phone call had us pack our bags might have been why April stayed with me to get the money. I didn't know she was that money hungry anyway, so we got on the road back to Cali. We drove the cars we had just recently got; when got there, we stayed at my mom's house. The next day I went to my aunt's house, alone in Compton, and I got the money she had called me there for. We had only been in California for a few days and the cars we came there with had gotten repo'd. They came and took our cars because we were told they didn't want them out of Arkansas. Within one week, April, the kids, Flower, and I were moving into a 5-bedroom house. I furnished the house and got April and I knew cars. I was 19 and showing everybody, I was a man.

Chapter 7

Wedding Bells

After shopping, at Walmart, April comes home with a wedding set of rings and says "Look!" "What's that" I asked, she replied "Oh, wedding rings were getting married, do you want to get married? "Sure," I said unenthusiastically, thinking I'm supposed to be down on one knee... "ummm, OK." Next thing I know I was in the Men's Warehouse with my brother, my cousin, and my stepdad getting sized for tuxes. We all purchase our tuxes and leave the store. That night I was allowed to have a bachelor party, the party consisted of all men I wasn't allowed to have a dancer. I wake up the next morning to get ready to marry April. I got up, I got in the shower and then I got dressed. The whole time thinking "What am I about to do?" After I got ready, I took one last look in the mirror and headed to the church. I stood there and I looked at the pastor, who was the same pastor from Aprils last marriage to Jello, all I did was smiled. He is still my friend to this day. From the start of April walking down the aisle to "You are now Mr. and Mrs. Ivan Edwards" was all a blur. I was now a married man at the age of 20, we had our reception following the wedding ceremony and it was held in the church parking lot. We had normal food, cake, dancing, and fun. I had my family and siblings all there. It was a nice day.

Chapter 8

The Family life

Even though I was young the family life was growing on me. Being married began growing on me. Still, I had an underlying feeling that something was all too weird about our situation. I loved April but I began to question was the marriage to hold me, so no one knew what was happening prior? I started pushing some bad thoughts out of my mind. Face value, the relationship was good, we didn't have any issues and like I said I began to love being a father figure and husband. We were living life as a married couple, while still figuring out how to handle our relationship and marriage. In the mist of everything

April started cosmetology school. Towards the end of her course, she tells me I can get my GED and attend the school as well. I got my diploma from Park Ridge High School in Long beach and started Marinello Beauty College. I took cosmetology classes because barbering class took too long. It ended up being a better decision because I learned everything. As you'll can see I mastered the re- twist on the first try. It took 10 months, and I graduated cosmetology School. After that I went to the state board and got my license. For a whole year we started doing hair out of the house. On one particular day there were 2 girls who came over, one lady was getting serviced while the other was just a tag along. The tag along was on the phone and at the end of the conversation both ladies ended the call saying "Bye Daddy" to the man on the other end. That intrigued April especially since she was into threesomes and such. "What was that about" says April "Oh, we share the same man," said the girl who was getting serviced. The tag along, in which we now know as "HER GIRLFRIEND", she said "It's called Polygamous" Aprils calls me down from upstairs and tells me about it and she asked me if I wanted to try it and I said no. For months she would ask me the same question and I gave the same answer. I only said no because I remember she would always show jealous ways and if I turned any way other than her way I would hear "why are you looking at her? Do you want to go live with her? or some weird remark. At this point

I didn't know if she was asking to test me or if her freaky ass was for real, but long story short, I ended up finally saying yes and she was making calls the very next day. April called a mutual friend of ours. A 27-year-old with 3 kids, she said no to the idea at first but just like me she eventually gave in as well, we went and picked her up and talked about some things and did something to and from there was the start of our first "poly relationship".

That was a trial run because it was very brief, there was a lot of jealousy in that relationship from April, she didn't like seeing anyone with me but her, the relationship had to go her way or no way I can tell by the conversations we had, with the ladies we met that introduced us to this lifestyle, "poly life" was a 3+ person relationship with an agreement as one, I think April had missed that concept. Even though that relationship didn't work out April wanted to try again.

Chapter 9

Foursome

April and I continued with the hair and managed to now own a salon, we both worked there. April got a call one day while we were at the salon it was an ex of hers from 10 years ago. He tells her that he wants to see her and checkup with her. He said he needed to ask her some questions, so I said that I didn't care and to tell him to come up to the shop. An hour after the call the ex, his baby mother, kids, and siblings all pull up to the shop and April gets scared thinking the worst. The details aint for you'll though, they ended up coming in and started talking, you know I had to have a smoke break.

I went outside to do what I did, after I came back in, I was told that we were about to drive 30 minutes away just to go to this man's family's house. I was confused because prior to that April was afraid to face these people, now it was like a big family reunion. Once we got to their place, I just stayed in the car and chilled and I let them reunite. After a few hours passed, April comes to me asking if I wanted to have a "foursome." I say "sure" thinking it's about to be us and two other women. I was informed that wasn't the case. April was now wanting to have intercourse with her ex and his baby mother, I turned that down immediately, but April was like "it's cool when you do it, but it's a problem when I do it" lol but no for real I just wasn't feeling it because it was a guy involved. I started to feel like April wanted to rekindle or see if there was still something between her and her ex. Once again, I gave in. I gave in to a swinger type deal. FUCK IT! Afterwards we went on about our night.

The next couple of days they were coming to BBQs at the house and hanging out, but an accident happened, and he ended up going back to jail. April made it her obligation to be his help on the outside so instead of him leaning on family and his kids' mothers he called on April. Me being the "husband" now puts me in the position to help and I wasn't feeling none of it I really had my I don't care attitude. The man had plenty of family, friends, etc. and so I had to ask her why she felt the need to insert herself so much. April's response "I don't care who got a problem with it I'm not leaving him to do this alone" during this time I got a word from a bird that she was going to leave me when he got out, so you know me, I had to get one up on her and go ahead and get out her way. Yeah, I left!

Chapter 10

Girlfriend

I packed my bags, filled my car up, and drove away. I went straight to my sister's house to crash for a while. Just until I figured some things out. The next day our girlfriend at the time had reached out to me and she said that she was told if she ever messed with me again she would no longer be able to be at the house, I said "are you ready to go"? she said "I'll be ok can you come and get me", so I did and we kicked it, after we were done kicking it next thing you know I'm dropping her back off at the house and April was up looking out of the window waiting and it was late too, she waited until our girlfriend went in the house next thing you know April snatched her phone out of her hand and found my number stored under daddy and she started beating her up.

April was F*****g the crip up the street 3 houses down, we will come back to that I don't know full details. I started getting messages saying all types of crazy stuff but that's not important right now. Let me get back to the story, I guess our girlfriend got away she called me to pick her up but I thought everyone was out to get me so I'm like nah I can't come, then she video calls me just to show me what's been done to her, so I went to pick her up and we got a room, we chilled, and talked about the situation. Next couple of weeks went by and I started getting messages from April saying come home, then besides that I would get pictures of me being at different places, I was like why are you stocking me? One day I'm at the gas station just chilling getting gas and April pulls up blocking my car in, she thinking I had gf with me ready to attack again, I just got out of the car, I left the whole car there and went walking through the field, she gets in my car, rip up my papers from the DMV and try to yank my steering wheel off. Two minutes later she drives through the field and taps me with the car It was nothing crazy I'm ok, but I was like what the F*** let it go. I called my sister and asked her can she come sit and watch this crazy girl. Mind you she got her daughter nagging it on making things worse but anyway she said "are you coming home? I'm like no! she says "where are your draws? I said dirty! she says "I bet! I said "me too, she says "you can go back to your car I'll leave you alone. I said cool. I got back in my car, and I went back to my sister's house to get some clothes then afterwards I went back to the room to chill for a while. My money started getting really funny, so I sold my favorite car for some pocket change. I still had to get another car to get around in and within a couple of days later I got another one, eventually it broke down on me now I was shit out of luck but there's always a ram in the bush at all times for me. I traded that car for an eclipse stick shift, I did not know how to drive a stick, but I knew a youngster would want the car, so I posted it for 1400 and it was sold the next hour. I went and bought an expedition an hour after that. As I was driving the truck, I was on my way to see gf and the spark plugs went out on me, so I sold it to junkyard for 250, which led me to be stuck in the middle of nowhere. I got a text that read saying "where you at? It was from April, I responded "I'm stranded! she replied back "I'll come get you I'm already in that area. I responded back I already have a ride coming! she says I'm pulling up that's when I said F*** it come on.

Chapter 11

Studsband

Now I'm riding with April and of course she's not going to take me to where I was, she took me back to the house and then boom she drops the bomb on me she said "I'm pregnant" of course I'm happy so I just said I'm coming home. I was working at a barbershop by my sister house so here comes April trying to get a job with me, I'm like sure I don't have no issues with it but if you are pregnant don't work too hard but come to think of it I have never seen no ultrasound nor pregnancy test, I guess she glammed me, I'll tell y'all about that later, so a couple weeks go by we working at the shop everything is going good then it was right back to the same ole stuff. April sees my phone there's a friend request from our ex-gf she calls her and says let's meet up and then she agrees.

April picks her up and takes her far out and asks her why she betrayed her? She says gf says she wanted her life she says wrong answer and cuts her hair off bald that was the last we heard from her.

April wants another gf but at this point I don't even care if it is what it is, so she gets on live on fB and asks who wants to be our gf putting out apps but this time she finds a stud who happened to live up the street from my grandmother in Los Angeles. They met on live and of course she asks me to drive an hour and 42 minutes away to go meet her which was ok she was nice and cool like me besides our birthdays are a day apart real Libra energy, so April moves her in, we try this thing out it goes smooth for a second then it started getting crazy out of nowhere. I think they wanted to be together alone and push me to the side. The study shows she was there for only April, so this wasn't beneficial to me. Of course, they're happy and I'm cordial and ok with it because I see it made April happy.

We started doing things together, but I felt weird because April wanted a husband on one side and "studsband" on the other side, me being such a cool guy the stud started showing more affection for me. I didn't know how to receive it because of the situation at hand but I also didn't want to be mean, so I began playing the role as "the studs' boyfriend" along with being April's husband. That relationship lasted longer than the first for sure, but it still wasn't what April needed obviously. She separated all of us and made a room for her new gf so she could go sleep with her alone and live they best life, but it wasn't so great she did whatever she wanted to do whenever she wanted and April says it's ok baby, I love you. I be like you got to be kidding me and that's the reason me and the stud would argue all the time, they will get serious, and threats come into play. I just be ready but April kisses her butt literally and they make up, but I take way longer to forgive and forget so it's like one sided. April has a husband and a studsband but I don't have a gf to be with me when she's upstairs for a week or down in La while I'm home by my lonely and nobody never seen a problem with that but it's ok I messaged a couple of people on snapchat just because I was bored and alone while April was out being with her studsband doing whatever in that trailer but it's all good, That was when I knew I was just there for security and protection just so she can say that she had a husband so I accepted that and it was like that for years.

Chapter 12

What about me?

One day Aril gets a call from our ex-gf saying how come she can't be with us like how the stud is, April says come home. April does a head full of hair, we chilled but the vibe 'was different for all but we tried it again, mind you there's a stud involved so it's like everything will be even but no it wasn't like that at all, April wants all the love so now all the attention is on April until it's time to smoke so when we walked off to go smoke or when we go to the room alone here comes April "what yall doing"? we replied "smoking." April then says "nobody's just going to lay up with my husband watching movies and smoking and leaving me by myself. "I said aint that some shiii, but we only got up and walked away so she can breathe because she has asthma but never used an inhaler, she would also sit up under her stud all day and night while she smoked day and night in a tiny room, but she can't breathe when I smoke. I don't understand it either so to be generous I tried to make it easier for her to breathe but it's a problem. Back to the relationship with all of us, it was ok, but a lot of the pressure was taken off of me and the stud was cool but not really because she would always do irritating things not on purpose that's just how she was, but I dealt with it when I wanted too and when I didn't I just didn't. I mean she could be in the same house, car, plane with me and I would not talk to her for a whole year. I didn't understand how April could keep her around all that time while we were really beefing and not speaking to one another, I would have sent her home but I'm not April. Any who she the stud and eventually she would get her shii together so I'll talk to her when she was in her right state of mind, I would even give her some sex but then the next day she goes back and do some crazy stuff which would turn me off completely towards her for another year. I remember one year it got so bad. I told April you can have your girlfriend if you want to be disrespected and threatened for your life all the time, cursed out, cheated on and whatever else you choose to deal with, you go right on ahead and do that. I said not me I quit forget all that. April says "ok but you not having your own girlfriend if that's what you were thinking I said "actually I've always been ok with just you she says "ok just letting you know. April and her girlfriend left for the day, they came back and went to sleep upstairs while I slept in the California king by myself. Moving forward everyone can tell that me and studdiana had issues on the lives, so it's like poor me but I didn't have an issue with it but in my head I felt the same way like what about me you know the guy you married which I find funny, am I even here? Do you see me anymore? But all in all, the ladies wanted to be around me just as much as they did her or if not more but April had to run the show.

Chapter 13

Who's Next?

Eventually everyone got tired of it we all wanted to be one happy family but that was not going to happen so I really just showed April all the love and talked to them whenever I could so basically they was my girlfriends when it was time to smoke or have intercourse which was barely so I stayed to myself which sure enough April ran the others away our old gf she had left again and I understand why, I mean we all supposed to be together but its giving one sided and like I said it was Aprils way or no way and everyone was getting tired of it the stud eventually left too and went back to La she got tired of

Aprils Bullcrap. I was like yes ok I got my wife back cool let's do this but that lasted briefly she would put up ads on the internet like who wants to be our Gf every app every day and it's like dang you do got a husband you don't have to have a girlfriend but she felt the need to want one so I'm like ok do what makes you happy and that's what she was going to do regardless. She started getting hit ups from some of the women who responded to the apps on the internet and she picked a couple of them to message back and meet up with if you ask me she was just thirsty for real but at this point so was I cause you hogging all the love but I aint tripping she never asked me about any of the ladies she would just show me a pic and I'll say oh nice next thing you know they'll be over our house trying to chill and get to know us but while we were doing that if whoever focus is not on April then it's a problem, the guest would go to the bathroom while they were in there April would tell me she doesn't want me that bihh aint gay she looking at you the whole time I'm talking to her all in your eyes and you not even paying attention to her I was like for real, she was like yea I want a bihh who like bihhs not who just want to F*** on my hubby. Long story short, most of those never worked out she would say give her what she came for and imma get rid of her. In my head I'm like you can't be serious but I'm not going to turn it down if that's what she came for but what if she wants more I feel they do come for a relationship some come to get famous lol, some come just to try to live a better life then they already had and of course we was poppin or whatever but it really wasn't like that more on the internet then in real life but they would have had to find out and of course at the time everyone who knows us was trying to get in where they fit in but everybody can't fit in this bed.

Chapter 14

She likes what she like

We tried; well, she tried, and she didn't stop looking. Everyone that wanted to be in a relationship it was like open access it was like April just wanted to be surrounded by women so she started responding to the messages, then eventually she would meet up to see if the vibes would be the same as the conversation they would have, just like the messages, which I never knew I was just the driver so she can meet them. I never said too much to them I might have offered a smoke maybe something to drink to be nice so a mf can be relaxed and comfortable if they choose to talk to me while smoking it's cool I don't have an issue but again April don't want nobody all in her hubby face for real so I tried not to do too much, she would always say "I don t want no friendly ass husband but what do you want me to do when you bring these women in my life, I never asked for any of it so the fact that I didn't I would like to get to know who I'm going to have any relations with or be in a relationship with because remember I didn't text or talk to none of them on the phone so when I got a chance I started a conversation whenever I could but as soon as I do here comes April saying why yall whispering I don't like that, so I go back to saying nothing cause it's pointless to start an argument over nothing when really nobody was whispering you just came back at the end of us meeting each other lol since we never talked. April says I showed you her, I said when that was and she said, the ass with the tattoo on it lol and of course I go ohhh yea now I remember. I said how am I supposed to know this was her and I didn't even know what her face looked like type shiii, you know what I mean so I try to be the nice guy that I am and start a conversation while smoking at least but it was always a problem. I began to just chill and if I got asked a question that's when I would say something, so I just continued to just wait for the night action to happen then go on about my night. Then it's like yall get out get up and go do something, yall not about to lay up and do nothing all day It's like I couldn't even relax and just chill because April had to be in control of everything so it made the women want to do their own thing like have an extra partner for back up just in case the "situation ship" with us didn't go as planned but April didn't like that she would say you can just go be with them now whoever you're texting, I be like just relax this why you don't have a gf now.

Chapter 15

Club Chic

The return of Christian who has been wherever he been, we'll all of the sudden he pops up asking to come over and hangout and tell us about whatever he has been thru so of course Aprils like sure come on over let me help you out in life, so he comes back and he's still the same infatuated mf he was back in the day. I pay it no mind he knows better than to play with me or whatever but he needs a place to stay and April volunteers our home, also our gf was almost out of the door because she was tired of her trying to be under me so she was trying to get rid of her without saying it so one day Christian says

I need some sex, and April says I have the person for you, use her as a practice run or whatever. This person happens to be our ex-gf. They do what they did or wherever and he comes back to tell me I didn't use protection my boy. I say oh you stuuupppiidd. A couple of weeks went by, and she calls to say that she's pregnant and he's happy as fuck, so cool, whatever, maybe they both needed that in their life I thought. Christian wanted the most he can get out of life with these females, so he always messed around on his new baby momma as she did him, so April says, but who cares long story short they're doing fine he's staying with us she's wherever she is. One day they decided to stay together the boy did something to her son on accident

I hope if it was on purpose he deserved everything that happened but yea whatever he did got him 5 years in prison, I was like dang that's wild, crazy, stupid and dumb but people do anything to get the mothers attention but um yea it wasn't sexual at all, he's just a dumbass individual period so now she has to have the baby alone of course. April wants to take care of everyone. She says I'll be the baby daddy you come move back in until you have the baby or whatever you want to do so she came back and stayed with us besides who wants to be alone during a time like this. April makes her comfortable just to tear her down again, she makes her feel like an idiot and tells her how dumb she was for leaving this for that but she orchestrated the whole thing it's beyond me but who was I? I minded my business just the driver at this point so that lasts for a while until it didn't anymore then it's off to the next. April just couldn't be without a woman or two or three mind you, yes, I'm still here, lol, but whatever you want happy wife happy life. So while her ex gf is back in the house April puts a new add up like the newspaper asking where's our gf with a picture of all 3 of us so some are intrigued some are not all that impressed but I never seen what her messages was looking like with these ladies so I would meet them when I see them it be cool vibes in the beginning until they say or do something not to her liking which would be an automatic dismissal like a dating show you would see on TV just not as many women as she wanted but none of them ever lasted not because of me I never kicked anyone out well maybe once I put her clothes on the deep freezer in the garage like you can for sure come get your stuff and leave quietly I'm not doing any yelling or getting upset and she did. I felt that was cool because others have to do the most to end a "situationship" but anyways when one leaves a new one comes so on to the next. One day we go to the strip club we met this lesbian couple in there and April she invites them to our house to chill, one girl comes the other she had to work so we chilling and the girl is rubbing on me like crazy like she was trying to get it poppin right there but I don't know what happened but she said she wanted it without her gf so we did it. Later the next morning

April tells her gf who was at work so now it's drama already the girl denies it, so April shows her messages I guess her gf began to cry and breaks up with her right there in the room. April says that's ok you can be with us and she can be with nobody so the gf who was at work was now our gf which was crazy I would've slapped somebody but that's just me so our new gf is ready for her session slash payback and Aprils ready to see what she was about because she was another stud she has been waiting for but she was also feminine asf so I guess that made her a fem is what the world say she was freaky asf for both of us but it felt weird like she had to please April just for me to please her if you get what I mean but I was cool. I feel she still wanted to be with her gf who was just kicked out the situationship honestly because she liked the intercourse we had, and it showed I was told by the person who put her up to it. One day April wants to follow her new gf like a stocker so whatever, she goes to her ex-gf house and gives her a couple things for her son like she maybe has been doing since the kid was born who cares April does and waits for her to come back to our house interrogates her, dump her and send her on her way.

Chapter 16

She's our girl now

Next couple of weeks I keep getting messages that I should smoke with this girl who used to be with Aprils daughter whaaattt yea but she was cool when she was around so I'm like whatever I'm close but I don't know, it feels kind of weird not only because she's Aprils daughters ex gf but more because she didn't talk to me like that when she was around but at the same time we smoked once before so I thought what the hell let me see what she wants. So I message her back like what's up she says "lets smoke but me thinking maybe she wanted to be in a relationship with us her and her new gf because we was in a relationship with a stud and her gf so maybe she wants to give it a try but I wasn't thinking that at the time but April was, so I asked April what did she feel about it since you know the situation. I guess she already been looking on their IG or at least the gf cause I told her about her wanting to smoke with me, she instantly says oh her gf is cute do they want to be our gfs I said no she just wants to smoke, she says "ok well yu get 'em instead of saying sure go smoke with them on their side of town since she don't smoke but she had to be in control of the smoke sessions as well. I went to pick them up and back to the crib we go, and the questions began. April asked "have yall ever been poly? do yall like couples? have you been with a man before? I haven't even broke down the cigar yet lol but that's how it be so they wasn't there for that but I think it was like more of a why not let's see what we can get outta this, what can they gain from us to better their life in general so they went for it or it could just be what was wanted from the first message to me from the one girl but idk and I never will but also I didn't care we was on how many ladies can we get. I guess that's how it was because here's come the girl from the strip club the one that got cheated on now, she wants to join all of us and I'm just like what the f*** ever cause April not going to want to do that but she did. Now there's 5 of us and it was working out plus everything was fine until one day Aprils daughter comes home and is furious and ready to beat up her ex gf which is our new gf lol I know, I know it's all crazy asf but anyway her mom doesn't let it happen, later she asked "why are you so angry! you told me you never liked her and never did anything with her so what's the issue but her daughter says I've told you multiple times she's who she lost her lesbian virginity too, I guess, idk maybe I think they argued it out. April says oh well I don't care I really like her gf. Anyways so watch what I do, I got this you made my daughter cry imma make you cry who knows what that meant so the next day the ex-gf goes downstairs and have a conversation with Aprils daughter apparently they kissed then boom there's the fuel April needs maybe it was a plan they're good for shh like that so April tells the other gf and she instantly breaks down and admits that this is why she didn't want to do this shh in the first place in case of old feelings popped up being that everyone was living together so she and April tells her that she has to leave so she does and her gf cries in Aprils arms all night so sad I was sad for real like that is so crazy that they would do that but then again the whole situationship is messed up mind you the old gf is back and she's lost and confused but that was Aprils favorite though so it didn't matter who stayed or left so ol' girl still crying she finally asked why you still crying, she says she misses her gf so she says she need to go home to clean her room so I say I'll take you cause I was still sad for her and she needed to get that room clean lol so I dropped her off. They was back together, everything was fine so that was cool back at the house it was just the 3 of us we were ok for a second but eventually she would get closer to me then before and start changing how she was I mean from jerseys to spaghetti straps lol I didn't notice at first but April did and called it out every time she did some girly stuff because she like that stud love but the gf like who she was becoming she liked the way I treat her so she would start to change for me and boy April did not like it so she called her out on it every time and one time gf said it's what she wanted to do she never said she was a stud honestly well she was kicked to the curb. The next couple of months she was pregnant God Bless her and the baby and now you would think we would have a piece of marriage to our self yea we did for about 2 days then she was bored with me again, I guess.

Chapter 17

Toxic

A year later here comes the stud coming trying to get her way back home saying that she's not doing too good, in Aprils eyes she was drinking a lot and doing other things that wasn't too good for her, so she says she wants her moved back in with us. I'm like here we go again but who am I, whatever do what you want like you always do, so she does, and it was like nothing ever happened. I was back alone in my room and April was back with her stud and I was ok with it for whatever reason so eventually she start asking me if I wanted my own gf I'm like yea sure but then again nah ill pass, you can't even handle the gfs you got so why add more when you obviously don't like them all on me, but if they were just for me like your studs are just for you then I should have but I wasn't even in to all of that for real. If it wasn't all of us, I didn't want to play around cause I know she already disliked it with a passion but it was done to me so I should have done it back but it's cool let's move forward.

The next couple of months ex gf wants back in again for the last time, far as my understanding. April tells me there you go now we can be even you got her I got my stud and I'm like whatever we might as well be in an open relationship. I often feel that April would think that I would leave her if I did have a gf on the side but honestly I think it would have been better to do it that way but she wasn't having it she had to run it all so even if I would have said yes it would have been weird I mean they would do it all, shopping, nails, movies, lay together, and ride together, but if I did it or say come ride to the store with me s*** would get crazy. I be like never mind maybe she wanted to get some things for herself, it was always why yall got to be sneaky? why we all can't go? I never said nobody couldn't go, I said out loud that I'm going to the store, which was literally 1 to 3 minutes away, but the jealousy was real, so I just took their money and grabbed what they wanted. When I would take their money that was even an issue cause April didn't know I took their money she always thought I bought it myself, but I just let her be mad and get over it later which she did only after she made sure it wasn't my money. She was my gf too so I didn't have a problem with it if it was my money or not it shouldn't have been no issue really whether everybody was getting along believe it or not. I still wasn't on great terms with the stud because of whatever reasons she was just not giving gf for me eventually she would start getting active with me and wanting intercourse from me but I'm like nah I'm cool, but April says how can you do one and not the other just to try and make me feel weird about it to my defense. One has on jeans, and one has on tights but whatever everybody gets naked let's figure this out and we did it and it was ok. We even shared and she put the plastic on, and I had the real thang. We did what we did. The stud, April, me and gf then we switched while they kissed. The stud takes the plastic off and throws it out the room then she bends over herself so I'm like ok teamwork make the dream work I got you. She fell in love with how I was making her feel and started wanting it more and more and more. I'm still not attracted to her like that and she still on my shit list, but a good night is a good night and that was it for now. Like I said she wanted more and started getting angry with herself because instead of asking or trying to join in she would just stay in her room and cry to April about it after telling April it should just be the both of them and kick everyone else to the side including me. April made it clear to her that nobody was having that, so she stayed upset most of the time. I wanted so much to just be loved but she just always did dumb things to turn me all the way off. I mean I wouldn't talk to her for a year straight and we lived in the same house she would come downstairs, come to me and April's room and stand in the doorway until April has to beg her to come lay with her but that mf couldn't stay still so she was up and gone. I would be watching TV, and she would say hi, I would ignore her, and she would say "I love you and walk off, she just didn't know how to be with a man, and it probably was never in her plans too but in order to be with April came me so eventually she grew more to me. We shared our bdays with each other and we did a lot until she would start stuff or April would start stuff with her and they began arguing over the smallest BS like her wanting to go to her family house it was an issue because of her past, I guess. April had a problem with more than likely everyone if they weren't there for her, so you know how that goes and here comes the arguments. When they would argue I was out of there and I'll go back to the house when they were done. When I got back, they were F****** I guess they ok now! Nope they would still argue over some dumb s*** oh well. The arguments would be so bad that I didn't want to talk to the stud because of the things she said to my wife, but she wanted to vent to me what am I to do so I listen. She is right, it's just the way she says stuff that turns me off, so I just stuck to myself like always. She ends up getting put out of the house cause of some other stuff and this time everyone's more into Facebook, so everyone wants to be seen. The stud runs to the internet starts all kind of crap calling me names which I didn't understand because the beef wasn't with me, but it is what it is she's doing the most and April feeds into it now. They would go back and forth day after day just to end up having her move back at the end and be back in love. That's when I knew she was toxic.

Chapter 18

Fugitive

Here is a new lady NuNu she was from another state I guess they talked for a lil bit on fb and FaceTime. I may have seen one conversation I didn't know the girl was on her way to our home, so we go ride to pick her up from the bus station, I guess. April got her a ticket and she came to the house of course they go live introducing the new gf that she just met so the viewers are all nice but one person notices her from home and says she's been through some things in life and we should just be careful but we brushed it off like ok whatever hater so ex gf calls and wants to meet her, see she stayed right up the street so she was with us whenever she wanted to be and join in when she wanted too which was fine by me. When someone new came around she made sure she did too, even if it was just to feel a mf out to see what they like and get tf on for a few weeks. This certain night she stayed, and some things went down. The next couple of days we got messages that the girl was going through all kinds of things and was on paperwork and wasn't supposed to be out of the state, so she was really running from the people in her hometown. The police showed up to our house asking for her and she was on the next thing smoking up out of there, I know crazy right she was 19 and still had a lot to learn. Now it's back down to April myself studdianna and half-time gf so we doing our thing living life going out every weekend and doing family events. I remember one day Christian calls from prison saying I'll be out in a week no longer than a month; we all been helping raise his son a little with his bm of course now she stuck at our house and don't want to go home. Studdianna didn't know him and didn't care but she heard about the dude. He wants to come stay with us when he gets out and he knows that we were having sex with his bm, but he thinks this is his opportunity to get in where he fit in saying we can all be together, nigga whattt! fuck no! fuck you stay in there for all I care. April said he can't stay there because she was a felon, and they can't live together basically you not about to be having sex with your bm in my house then she still wants to be with us so that would have been weird. That's what they wanted I believe but I wasn't on that at all, they had to figure something else out he still wanted to come to our house to see his son so April agreed to pick him up, but he couldn't stay with us.

Chapter 19

Drama

Today is the day the boy gets out of prison with nobody to pick him up because of the bridges that he burned with everyone, but he still had that middle school mindset to where he thought everyone was playing with him. It wasn't a game, and he needed some serious help and that wasn't my problem, I didn't feel sorry for him because he was still very much infatuated with April and everyone in jail knew it. I mean when some of my homies from my barrio hit me up and tell me that n****s are in jail saying that they had sex with my wife, I'm like whattt oh matter of fact I already know who it is and they said yea he was a weirdo he used to beat on his self to make people think he was scary but that didn't work he still got beat up for doing dumb stuff the whole time that he was in there. Yea he is getting out today, let's go pick him up. He was only 30 minutes away his baby mother made sure she was there at the house when we got there, she was happy but sad and confused about wtf is about to happen. When we got back to the house, I'm paying attention myself to see her reactions towards him she started recording him walking in the house as he cried seeing his son for the first time. What a moment it was and a great feeling I bet, he started bonding for a second and he acted as if he didn't see his bm. He waited until everyone was not paying attention, she slides off to the garage next thing you know he's gone as well so hmmm. We walked in the garage he has her in his arms holding her like he missed her, and he acted like they were at her house but that's still Aprils Gf at the time so she slaps her and ask why tf are you in his arms she says I just wanted to see if he can still pick me up. In my head I'm like his height is 6,3 and he weighs 280, just did 5 years in prison, he been picking men up so stop playing. April says show me how it happened so he picks her up again, April doesn't like it and tells her she can leave while he is still there, he has to find somewhere to go as well because parole and me smoking didn't mix. I didn't want them going through my stuff whenever they felt like it, so he had to go too. He searched around for a couple of days and still had no luck, so he did the craziest thing I ever heard, this mf asked my mother, and I said my mf mother and he didn't tell anybody. A couple of days later I found out and I'm like Hell NO! We are not doing that. I told him to get tf out of there before I came over there. Him and my sister dated before in the past when they went to school together so she must have felt like they were going to be together because she told me that he didn't have to leave. I told my mom, and she said that I don't pay no rent there which I didn't, and I wasn't about start so I fell back. April on the other hand was more upset and wanted to take a trip to my mother's house and talk to them face to face so we did and when we got there guess who was there at my mother's house you guessed it, yea it was him with his bm our gf lol whatever, but they were just chillin. April got so upset jumping in my mother's face like she was about to do something to her, but she just threw the car keys across the floor and said don't none of yall call me when yall need me. Sure, enough she was needed I don't know what happened, but we had him back in the car again. We picked up his new gf that he was already beefing with I don't remember how we ended up over my mom's house, ohhhh yea he was messing with a dude, his baby mama broke the window to see who it was in there and she said that it was a man or a big girl with hair on her face. She jumped through the window they took off in the car. My mom was out of town when all of this happened. April says hold on I'm coming which we were chilling with his new gf because we were all friends first before he got out, but he was on I want everybody type s*** which I couldn't blame him. We were outside I don't know why but this ninja picked her up by the throat, threw her on the rocks in the front yard and choked her until she passed out, I said wtf this mf going back to prison but nobody called though, I said whaaatttt that's crazy the other girl never got out of the car she was terrified I guess but she ended up having a baby later by him so she wasn't too scared lol but that's irrelevant. I guess not hold on, so we went back to our house and the one gf Ubers home, and the baby mama comes in to the room get held and cry a little and says bump this let's have intercourse so we did. April myself the bm and studdianna so while I have them on top of each other doing my thing looking at the booties a light fly across the room really fast I pay it no mind being that there's a street behind the house maybe it was a car turning. I kept stroking boom there's another light and that's when I immediately knew that it was his crazy ass in my backyard, so I finished and stepped back and said your baby daddy outside man. They all said, "how you know I said trust me and I looked and said yes, this ninja is standing outside all he was missing was the radio. April says what are you doing in my backyard he says he deserves to be up there I'm like whhhaaatttt for what because remember he still infatuated with April as well so he's like he's doing her, and I could be doing you too. April not happening I don't care what he thought. I think April would have said yea just because but whatever so he's down there apologizing on and on, I started rolling up my blunt he says to the bm what I got to do to show you I'm sorry this mf says let me put the studs strap on and do something to you right now I say whhhatttt tf and I told them to get the f*** out of here. This mf said yes to her, and they went upstairs, and they did what they did. April helped the stud record, I left and waited until they were done. When I came back to the house, they said that man pooped I said yall some weird nasty mfs but he did just get out of prison, so it probably wasn't nothing to him but yea he walked back wherever he came from. They talked about his shitty ass all night the fact that April helped him is beyond me. You'll do anything to use something against a mf someday. Moving forward he had a baby with the other girl who watched the bm get choked slammed. They are driving one day it was a year later in another state, and this boy driving 110mph he got pulled over and goes right back to prison for the choke slam that he did on his bm. I guess she did tell on him, so now she stuck in another state with a newborn baby. She needs help, she calls April, but nobody helps her, she had to figure it out. BM goes back home to her people up the street. Now it's time to visit Houston TX for the first time, Studdiana doesn't want to go because of some bs reason so we go without her. April calls her on valentine's day no response all day so April hollers its over blah blah blah so studdiana do not care because she's doing her own thing and free from us and the drama. Studdiana messes around and cheat on April/us with her ex-gf god mother and let it be known she was something different and didn't give a f*** that April was her gf, she wanted what she wanted so she pursued.

Chapter 20

Mixed Emotions

This girl was something different she was in love with studdiana and didn't care about who she was with where she lived or nothing, she made sure she was going to be around and hold her down which she did so before we got back to Cali, they had a whole relationship I mean she went and stayed with her on valentine's day and I guess it was over from there so why not live your life like you wanted so they did. She started moving her stuff out while we were gone. She came back and got the rest of her stuff and then she was gone. Afterwards she gets on the internet, goes live and talks a bunch of s*** all because they argued about nothing but yet she goes live and make it bigger than it is so here she go again throwing me in the mix of the drama. It's always her downplaying my manhood or calling me something I'm not, once again I cut her off, I didn't care what she said about me at this point, she just mad at April right now and she's still an emotional female with relationship issues that she has to work on and for her being a stud I'm sure it was hard, she made it hard. I guess with her I did play a part in not wanting to be intimate with her but when I was, I did beat the lil thang down and she loved it more then I knew. Anyway, they moved to Vegas for a better life or whatever I guess that didn't work out too well but that's their business. One day we went to

Vegas just to chill, well that's what I thought and as soon as we got there April says guess who's out here? I say "let me guess your stud, she says "how did you know? I say "I didn't but why are we here? she says "I just want to check on her and make sure she's ok. It was about 2am when they were on the phone she said "if you want to see me, I'm outside on this street. April wastes no time she wakes me up and says "let's go see her. I'm like for what? She's in a relationship aint she? She says "I don't give a F*** I want to see her. I say, "whatever let's go man. It's in the middle of the night but we in Vegas nobody sleeps but me lol, so we left, go to a gas station, we met up with her and her cousin. They talked for hours about the same ol' stuff she's talking big crap about the girl she's with really bad but staying with her, so I don't know how that works. April says I want to meet her! she says for what? She says I just want to see if she looks better than me, so she says well I'll let you know by tomorrow so then she does. We pull up, they met, and her gf doesn't like April but does want to be cool but studdy didn't want it that way because now they can double up and talk about her knowing I don't too much give a F*** about none of it. I just sat back and observed everything, she tells us about her messing her car up already and some other things that's not for this book, so long story short stud's new gf want some of old gf and have a night. I'm like whhaattt this can't be, but it was, and it took a minute, but it happened and that's when they messed everything up because after that she always wanted to be around and try to join in on the fun lol not after the way the first time went down and the way that it made her felt. I guess studdy felt some type of way because her feelings were stronger than I thought so she told her gf that she can never mess with her old couple again because she will not allow it so she gets upset, they argue fight and some more stuff than leave and go back with their life.

Her gf is not done with us she wants round 2 with or without studdy so she gets it one way or another. Oh, studdy is mad now everybody is a bag of B****s but remember she did it first so oh well. April tells stud we about to be together all 4 of us, she says oh Heck nah ill beat her up before I let her join us, so she does it just for payback but was right back in her face after all of that. April tells her nah we can't be together but studdy doesn't want to hang with April anymore. She's not mad at me you know cause I um, ya know what never mind. April was very upset with her because she said no lol so studdy leaves with her new gf and they go to La from Vegas. We lived in the city in between so the day we got back, they're on live talking crap about April so April is about to be on her way to LA to confront them. I don't want to go but for support just in case some s*** got real, I had her back. I knew studdy wasn't going to let anything happen, but you never know so we drove down there. I sat in the car for a second just to make sure there's no bs. I took a ride to my grandmother's house up the street so I could hang with my brother until they were done. Which can be the next day messing with them, I should've gone to the strip club every time she chased her gfs. I should've looked at booty jiggling since I had to be up all night but nah, I was up and outside their house in the car sleeping so I didn't have to hear the s***. April calls me and says "come get me but I'm still sitting in the car for another hour like be so for real right now. April says I'm not messing with her no more she can do what she wants to do I don't care. Right after that night, April phone rings, you have a collect call from STUDDY, call accepted, she's crying, I'm going to hurt myself! I don't want to be here can you please come and get me? April looks at me, I look at April and say it's your money do what you want to do so she drives 2am and go bail her out. We waited until 6am she gets released at 7am they about to go to sleep of course. April is too tired to drive home so she stays in the trailer with studdy for the night and I'm alone in my bed trying to sleep but this that toxic s*** they love so whatever they'll be arguing soon so I thought.

Chapter 21

Bye Cali

April tells me now that the bail bonds said that she has to worry about her every move like she's a baby and I mean her every move so of course she has to move back in and be separated by herself and have her own room again. Same stuff different house and yes, her ex-girlfriend is still on the phone with her everyday while April sitting right there, she does not care, well none of them care about nothing they had going on it was already too much going on but there all here for it. Now studdy is being mean to her ex instead of them being how they were, maybe it was because she didn't bail her out instead April did. Maybe April feels studdy owes her a relationship now since she was the one who got her out so April uses that and reminds her every time that they argue like "I could have left you in there and she says "you could have but you didn't so stop bringing it up if you love me! It is crazy to bring it back up anyway, like who wants to be reminded of that every time but then again who wants to argue all day, I know I don't that would drive me crazy every day. Anyway, so now it's time to go to Texas again, this time studdiana wants to go, we are going to look for a house so she wants to go now so she can see what her room is going to look like. April wanted to move to Houston because her fan base was 95% Houston and 5% Cali so why not leave and see what it's like. April had no family in Cali so why stay so she wanted to move it's like we had no choice regardless of our family still being there, but it's ok it gives us more options for content cause TX is so big so it's like we should do crazy videos. I knew the car scene was big out there so why not let's give it a try, we planned the trip, and we flew out there. We stayed with a friend when we got there because they offered and besides their home was really nice. They had picked us up from the airport, they even had great hospitality, I'm talking about they were some really cool people. Now it's time to look for houses, we said that we will stay for 1 month and if we find something cool and if we don't, we don't. 29 days go by we found something the last day and it was just right and in the right neighborhood.

Chapter 22

Texas

We got the keys, now it's time to move from California so we left Texas, and we fly back to California to go pack up the house, get the cars and say our see you laters to everyone after we were done, we got on the road. I drove the soul pack and April rides with studdiana, we get to Texas, and we move everything in. April leaves the house in California to her daughter and her gf to see how she can handle it on her own yea that lasted for a short time, so we are in Texas now living good, it's a real nice neighborhood, no crime, no problems well April and studdy still arguing all the time. I guess the arguments would be about me and why I don't treat her as I would anyone else, we have been with. I would ask her like are you going to change for me? wear a thong? let your hair down? take the collared shirt off? put some leggings on and dress like a woman? She couldn't do it and I wasn't going to force her. That's not who I am it doesn't even matter, but it was just weird all the time, we would have the same outfit on kissing, or you want to take a picture sagging with a hat on like just to let it go it's ok lol. To be honest she was feminine for me on camera and off camera, it didn't matter, and she didn't play about her man even with April, she would tell her that's my man with his fine assss and April would say girl that's my husband what are you talking about, lol, in the middle of the argument. I always stayed out of it but stayed right there to make sure they wouldn't fight but the most they did was argue everyday it would make me upset because if yall have to argue then yall don't need each other. Why keep on keeping on with the same stuff which I finally think April seen for herself that she was getting tired of the disrespect from her, so she says but didn't really do too much about it, so she continued to do it. Eventually it was time to get out and see what's up, we were invited out a lot and we went to a lot of different restaurants and events where everyone knew who we were, and it was nice. Of course, someone was always trying to get a gf, so we went to a bbw strip club, and it was the first one that I've ever been to. They flocked like birds on seeds, there was this one that she liked more than the others she invited her for a night of fun. The girl wants to be in a relationship with us but studdy says nah we not doing that, I'm like she doesn't run anything, but I guess she did I didn't care though. I don't even think about it like that, poly that is and to me it's a lil playdate or PPA as April calls it. What is that you might ask oh it's a planned pusssssy appointment I guess, plan it out, do it and it's done simple, but everyone wants to be in relationship just for them to fail over and over why I don't know. I always thought because they wanted me more than her and she wanted them more than me she would tell me all the time you married a lesbian sorry oh well. I would say I'm a lesbian too just not a whore lol, but I was in my mind, and I would look for attention on snap everybody had they booty out lol. I didn't see a problem with it since she was up her gfs assss all the time why can't I look at some it was better than me actually having a gf to myself in a separate room and going back to my wife when I'm done sexing whoever is in the room alone. It all sounds crazy yea I know like why you would come back in here and ask for some sex like you weren't getting plastic all night, I don't want it why don't you go back to your gf smelling like plastic and cigarettes and some other stuff I can't even think of right now. It was annoying and was giving fake asf then afterwards she would sleep for the whole day like where tf is breakfast lol but being the nice guy, I would wait every day until 7am to 4pm for breakfast. All because she had to go live getting ready for 4 hours or just want to lay up and do nothing until it's about that time or wait on studdy she's never ready. I would just go grab some donuts to hold us over after I dropped kiddo off at school because I know how the mornings are going to go. I'll get on live for 2 hours trying to kill time, chop it up with yall for a little and see what yall got going on. Everyone would ask me what was for breakfast? I'm like sigh nothing, April wanted to try new restaurants often which were cool, but she wasn't getting the content she should have so it was all pointless. The food was good though! Studdy and I are on ok terms, we smoke outside waiting for food to get ready she often tells me she loves me and that she did care about me. She just didn't know how to show it for real because she never had a man, I accepted it and moved on. Things were getting better now; April wants a new gf or two, so this couple invited us to a party with 2 wives, so we went it was a nice lil event and they were cool, so we invite them over to hang out. They hung out for a while, we all got to know each other, they wanted to join us, we said sure they say ok, and they left. 10 minutes later they called like we might as well get it cracking, I say whhaaatttt already, oh well, I guess. I know what's about to happen, so we did it and they came back a couple times we went to their place a couple times but of course it didn't last long, I don't know the reason but who cares not me so now it's back to us 3. I don't know why that wasn't enough for April she still tried to get as many women as possible, but they just weren't with it for real plus its always drama on live who wants to be involved in that then play like it isn't anything going on that's crazy.

Chapter 23

The Daughter Ex

We are on our way; we took a trip to California where we had to go and save the daughter. We left her the house in California and after a couple of months she let the house down literally. She had crap on the floor, the dogs had their own room, it was holes in the wall, the backyard was full of trash, the garage was full of trash, it was just too much going on. We went to visit, and I didn't want to sleep there at all, but they couldn't do what was needed so it had to be shut tf down immediately, so we packed their stuff up and I had it all cleaned up. We got on the road back to Houston and moved them in with us. They got their own room so now it's time to grow and be happy and live their life. Well, her girlfriend at the time used to have a girlfriend and she wanted to come visit them, so she did, and she chilled with them as a girlfriend but all honesty they treated her nicely. Eventually they had a night and I guess everything went crazy, they would argue all day and the girl would come down the stairs and sleep on the couch by herself after being in her feelings and when they would come down, they would make food for them and leave her on the couch hungry. I would have gone home honestly but she stuck it out they fixed it but only for so long because it was just too toxic because of inner feelings between the other two from the past so back to the couch she goes. One night we went to this party, April and I and somehow their girlfriend was invited since she was on the couch, so she got ready, I drove. We got to the party and April said her back hurt the girl says ill rub it which she does I don't know the movements, but it looked like a hunch while rubbing. I paid no mind, it was none of my business really, so they were done with that, so we went to the party it was packed full of people, you know me I'm ready to smoke 1. I was only allowed to smoke in the garage which was small and also packed so April couldn't breathe remember so she goes outside, and the girl goes with her. I sat and chilled it was 40 minutes later, I slide outside and boom they're kissing I'm like wtf is going on but yet still none of my business. April does what she wants when she wants so I'm ready to go now. We drive, we get to the house, the other two who were at home not even knowing she was gone are downstairs waiting for whatever reason not knowing the girl had already told the situation to her first girlfriend. April says we gone' stick to nothing happened and she says I aint gone say nothing I got you. They walk in our bedroom the little one says you kissed my mom she says yup then boom they are going at it now the other one jumps in boom. The momma/girlfriend breaks it up and tells her daughter to get out and tells their gf to stay in the room which she doesn't. As they were leaving the daughter ran into the garage and gave home girl a clean one to the eye it got low fast, but she was alright she didn't hit back because she just started a new relationship now with her mom, so she shook it off and relaxed. I smoked with her and relaxed with her a little bit, but she was still angry, so April held her. I went about my business watched a movie and was just thinking about how crazy all that happened. April and the girl go upstairs to studdy's room and chill with her I guess they got horny or whatever. I woke up and they are telling me how them 3 did the nasty, I'm like whaaaattt ok that's cool I guess then she says yea she's going to be our new girlfriend. I'm like ok whatever I guess she's cool and while I was getting to know her, she was starting to talk and grow a little on me. April's daughter says she needs to come get her stuff, studdy says ok cool I'm about to beat her girlfriend up she talks too much crap on the internet for her. I guess they had their own beef going on as studs so when they came before they pulled off, they rolled up the street they turned around and studdy was outside talking. April's daughter hopped out to study and said OK you can get it first and before she could run up, she sprayed her with mace, put it back in her pocket and drove off lol I didn't see it but that's what I was told. I missed it by a second just by the hair on my chinny chin chin. The new girlfriend comes out of the room and says that's why she didn't go out there. She said she already knew how they were coming, so she poured milk and all the stuff to make it stop burning on studdy. The next day we continued like nothing ever happened, I'll go live and smoke my cbd. I'll often smoke with both gfs, it's no problem but when I smoked with gf #2 alone it would be in the garage, we would try to wait for studdy but yall know how she do takes her time she would get left out sometimes so it'll just be me and gf and we will get to talking about a little of nothing just getting to know each other. Here comes April on that same s***, "what yall talking about? us "nothing really just smoking so she says why yall get quiet when I come In. (DEJAVU) here we go all over again, "I only got quiet cause you stated talking, just come in here and sit in this smoke and listen and she does with an attitude, so it kills the whole vibe. I go to the room they go upstairs with studdy eventually gf comes down to see what I'm doing which I was doing nothing besides watching tv, she joins as if she was in an actual relationship with me, like she should. She then lays with me under the cover, I put my hand on her booty then boom April comes in and her eyeballs on fire. She almost choked on her water and say "come on get up we bout to clean up aint nobody bout to lay up with my husband which I heard that before. I already knew where this was going so April says let's go to the mall so of course I have to drive. I go to gf and April argues over the dumbest thing about where the car was parked or something. April says I'm about to buy her ticket and send her back to California, she gets it but cancels it after they talk it out. The next morning, she made breakfast it was some stuff that April didn't want so she felt like she made it just for me, I didn't know and didn't care, I just ate it and went back to watching my movie. Later that night April says I'm sleeping with studdy tonight you and gf can sleep in our bed but please don't do nothing sexual, I'm like whattttt but you about to be doing you, why I can't but if I did it was called cheating, so I didn't even cuddle I just went to sleep. A couple of days later she reversed it and said studdy sleeps with me and gf sleeps with her in studdy room, but she didn't say don't do anything in fact she said please give her some she really needs it, that's all she talks about in that room. I said no I'm cool but studdy did her own stuff she backed that lil pancake up, pulled her boxers down lol and layed there and sigh and say you aint gotta be scared this the best you ever had then she said f*** me like you f*** me. Then I'm like huh, she said "yea stop playing you know you want this, I'm like who me I just want to go to sleep but I'll give you a lil sample then go to sleep. Afterwards she leaves to go and smoke a cig, but she never comes back lol they all sleep up there in her room I didn't care but I did. Oh well who was I right. A couple of weeks went by April wants to send gf home so she can fix things with her daughter, but her daughter gf is not feeling it she still isn't trying to see eye to eye and wants blood lol jk, she's still angry but she would get over it soon. Now that ol' girl is back in Cali they momma all they got.

Chapter 24

Surgery

April been wanting surgery for the longest she finally got the opportunity, so it was off to Mexico we go. Her surgery was the next day they prepped her for the procedure and of course I was the only one there for her in Mexico for 4 weeks, the real Mexico over the border, Tijuana Mexico. I'm like oh nah this not where I want to be, but I had to be the man for April cause studdy wasn't doing that, she was a stay-at-home stud but man they cut this lady tf open and some more s***, and I mean like it was scary seeing all that meat just sitting on the table. I'm scared asf that they didn't put her back together the right way, it was like why not just workout but whatever let's get you back walking and feeling better. It was crazy it was so much fluid, I had to wipe her from the front and back and help her out, it took 4 weeks for her to be able to really feel a little better and good enough to fly back home, just had to throw that in there. Why did she say that I didn't do anything for her? It's a lot more but we are going to leave that right there. So now it's April 1 and studdy and all the ladies that wanted to link with us or hang with us. Studdy wasn't with it and if she didn't want it to happen, April made sure that it didn't happen for the satisfaction of her studdy but did not even think that maybe I'd like some company as well. To me studdy didn't want me to have any company either, I think she was starting to want me for herself, and it was starting to show more and more on and off of the internet. When I tell yall she was really trying to be my lil b**** and I was like ok get your female on lol but April on the other hand would talk down on her for doing it and try to pull her stud card. April didn't care for me but for her instead so studdy would turn up and say oh well b**** you just mad because he wants to do me lol and this the best Puusssyy he ever had that's why you don't want him F******* me. Now April is in defense mode, and she tells her "Girl I don't care! Then she would be like he wants you gone but that's yo man yea right. Then says how he yo man when you just told me you want me to yourself last night! Now here they go arguing again. They end up going upstairs for hours so I go live and talk to my fans and see what they are up to. April comes on my live to check the woman who are talking to me then goes back to doing what she was doing, it's like why you would even come in here making things difficult with people who I will never see that's pointless! let them women flirt like they flirt with you all night and day what's the issue. It's cool when they do it, but it's a problem when I do it, whatever moving forward. April is getting bored with studdiana and she'd rather start a big fight with her over nothing over and over blaming it on me which I did have something to say a lot but studdy would always be like ok and just do what I tell her to do well almost because she was still hard headed as a mf which why we bumped heads. I had love for her and just wanted the best for her to be honest, but she didn't for herself in my eyes which made me upset in my heart because she had a lot that she wanted to do, and she had the mindset to go for it but didn't have the drive for it. She needed a push to keep pushing so she would often talk to someone about whatever she's going through and would make April mad because how can you tell a stranger all your business but not your girlfriend lover so that would happen a lot. April grew tired of the constant disrespect from studdy and kept threatening to kick her out, studdy got tired of getting threats to get kicked out so she found a friend who lived around the area and started to hang out, go to the beach have lunch and I guess to have a good time or whatever that was. April acted like she didn't care honestly; she was ready for her to go so she could start a new relationship.

Chapter 25

It's finally over

Let's get to it, the next day we had company over, the Yotts who would come over a couple of times a month and hang with us. They are some real cool people well on this particular day April and studdy have not been speaking to each other and you know I wasn't really messing with her like that on and off for the most part. On this particular day they come over and want to know why studdy is not hanging out so one of them goes to her room upstairs and checks on her. I guess she was not in her right mind, she was faded off the locos as she would call it and she happened to do the worst thing she could have done to me because I was so hurt about this situation, I even blamed the kids for taking it all this time. 3 years of me searching high and low telling her about it and her knowing she had it just did it for me, so Yotts comes down frantic and devastated she says quote "I don't know if you guys know but studdiana has a firearm up there! and I'm like yea her little pellet gun she got from Walmart it's no big deal it's not real everything is ok. She then says no I'm pretty sure it's real, I say "how you know? She says it's not the pellet gun it's a black revolver with long gold bullets in it. I say whaaattttt! She says yea she had it in a safe under her bed wrapped in a bandana. I said shiny black? She said no its matte black with a black handle. I say that's my s*** that's been missing, and I had reported it stolen over 2 years ago. Then she said the serial numbers were scratched off and everything. I say no way! She says I can show you just get her away from the room unquote then boom studdy asked me for a ride to the store. I told April to take her, so they left. Me, and her god mom go to find the safe and the key was under the bed, we opened it up and sure enough wasn't s*** in there so I checked the other ones, and it was nothing. Studdy hid it somewhere not knowing if she can trust yottie. Now I'm looking around both her rooms, why did she have 2 rooms and neither room was with us, but she was in our relationship. I'll never know to April studs run the world and get whatever they wanted hell she wrecked 2 of April cars then was blessed with her own and wrecked that to not to mention the one in California before we moved and her ex-gf car. She just didn't need a car anyway, back to the story at hand. I find nothing so now I'm tripping but I definitely believe her because wtf I been looking for it forever so I simply text her and said can you show me what you showed her because how come I didn't know you had a gun. I took you to the shooting range! Why you didn't bring your own gun? Where did you get it from? you know I just wanted to know, then she says I don't know what tf you are talking about! so now I'm getting upset cause this lady is not about to lie on you about some s*** she has no knowledge of. She says that's why she was sitting here fake smiling in my face to run back and tell my business. I thought more of she feared for her safety yall know studdianna crazy, so she kept denying it. I say it's all good just don't ask me for anything and don't talk to me at all! I have no words for you. I could have gone crazy on her and just made her give it to me but I'm not that type of person I'll let God handle it. Instead of her telling me here's your stuff I'm sorry I love you because that's what she should have done and gave me my s***, she texted me back and says can you get me a U-Haul? I say nah I can't get you anything, definitely not in my name so mind you her and April were still not seeing eye to eye but she took her to get the U-Haul just to help her out. They argued the whole way there but not about my gun being stolen she still angry about the other girl that she left with that one day so they are arguing and studdy says b**** ill end your whole life so April being in fear for her life she tells her to get out and leaves her at the U-Haul place hoping she didn't get a U-Haul but she always finds a way and got her a U-Haul. Studdy was back at the house before April and just started packing her stuff up mind you it took her 10 hours yall, remember I sat right there as she went up and down the stairs for 5 hrs on live then had a phone call and got right back on live for 5 more hours. She took her time as she should then she had the nerve to even ask me for help like I was going to say yes, right before she even started packing the U-Haul, she had someone pull up, she put the safe along with two bags in the car and the lady sped off. I'm guessing that was the firearm so back to sitting while she packs her stuff she's walking back and forth on the phone talking like I'm supposed to care saying and this mf just sitting here and won't help me, he just chillin and smoking on live. I'm like yup, you're right and I'm not helping you with anything. After 10 long hours she drives off into the night with nowhere to go, oh yea who was the lady in the truck? I guess that's where she went because she was good for a couple of days. April gets a message that said "come get your girl, she's annoying and she stole from me. I looked at her and said nah I can't help her, but April says I have too she has nobody else. I say oh well you go help her don't bring that s*** back over here!

You deal with it and if you bring her back, I'm leaving. April still goes and she got her hotel for a month and paid for it how dumb right? So of course, she says imma go stay with her there for like a week to make sure she's good and got food. Of course, she'll make any excuse to stay away from me and be back up under studdy since she's not with her new ex gf anymore. She wanted her back even though she stole from us. Yes, us I brought April a 2500 charm she took it off in her room and never seen it again when she woke up. 3 months later I'm minding my business at the pawn shop looking for a deal I see the charm with no question that it was it, I asked them about it, and they knew who it was, knowing she came in with me before, and tells me exactly when she came months back and how much she got for it. I told April she said I figured that and let it go and stayed with her, I would have dropped her then, but she didn't care once again. April still stayed in that room with her until she disrespected her live with over 2k views, so she got up and walked off and never looked back finally that was the end of studdianna for April.

Chapter 26

She's A fling

Well, well look at here it's back to April and I for like a week then out of nowhere she finds a new girlfriend of course a stud just for her again. I didn't even know about it until the day before, when she went to pick her up from the airport. I'm like ok it's your world, you do what you want anyways but she let me know that she's for sure not for me she's a real stud that's on some touch me not type s*** or whatever tf that means. I told her that I didn't care, so April picks her up, they go eat, then come home. The girl walks in and says hello I'm kyky she then extends her hand for a hand shake just to show acknowledgement of her new girlfriend's husband and that's it and that's all. I was ok with that I guess but thinking she was going to be weird to me she actually wasn't she was cooler than I thought, she wanted to watch movies with me and have a shot while I smoked, that was cool. We even played pool. It was like me having a lil home girl from my neighborhood, she was from LA as well but on the other side from where we were from, it was all good though. We were cool April would stay upstairs with her at night and they would go out as a couple, I wouldn't want to go because I wasn't really in a relationship with them at all so why go, I'll be ok in my room. Did yall have a great time? I asked when they came back, April was ready to get in their bed upstairs, kyky wants to hang out have a shot or two with me and chill so this was a short relationship. I guess she came to get info, she wasn't really into April like that her ex-girlfriend sent April messages of them talking about using April and that they were still in a relationship, and she would be leaving soon. All I could do was laugh to be honest cause ha-ha wtf lol so April said let me help you get out of here and got her a ticket back home it happened one of them days while I was at work at the jewelry store, and I didn't even get that goodbye handshake lol but whatever God Bless and goodbye finally I got my wife back, right? Buzzer sounds wrong.

Chapter 27

The last live

Now I'm sure yall like finally they are going to just do them and be a happy monogamous married couple umm nope, April has been talking to this new stud name Bentley who stayed in Michigan, I seen her talking to her before when she had her other stud so I'm not thinking anything of it but then it went from texts to calls from calls to FaceTime from daytime to overnight from a couple minutes to a couple of hours, then from a couple hours to overnight from overnight to the house. Whhhaatt, I know right lets back this up so she would text this person all night telling her whatever she felt comfortable telling her and not knowing her intentions she used everything for her advantage. Eventually she started calling and having conversations. April would sometimes show me on the phone, and she would make a stink face and look away then say "I called for you why am I looking at this n***a, can you get me off the phone with him. I'm like dang what I do not knowing that April over here bad mouthing me to her and downplaying me as a man, basically telling her whatever she needed just to get under my skin when it was time for her too. I didn't have an issue with her, I was really thinking that everything would be fine, but it wasn't for real they played tf outta me, even if they didn't play me, why would you let someone that you know come just to cause problems in your marriage. I would have never done her like that, she even asked how I would feel about them getting married but me thinking that she's just messing around playing she wasn't. Then she went on saying that the stud wants to get married before she died and it's all she wanted to do all these years, but it never did happen. I'm like oh ok if there's any law to where yall can get married for 2 days or something that's cool lol, I guess they ran with that s***. When I tell you they stayed on FaceTime all day and night not caring if I was sleep or not, I guess that was the best time because I couldn't hear a thing, but she definitely disrespected me the whole convo. I woke up at 6am to take her son to school. All she wants to do is go to sleep. I'm like girl get up and take him to school but after being up all night on the phone she was finally tired, only because the stud had to go to work, I guess, and that's when she got tired and fell asleep. By the time I'm back from dropping him off which I did his whole middle school and high school days just so she can sleep peacefully. I never had an issue with taking him to school, besides who wants to ride with their mom? I made the ride fun and gave his friends rides too so it made him even cooler. Back to what I was saying by the time I got home she's already back on the phone because the stud couldn't do anything without her and by me listening to their convo it was giving controlling, obsessed and delusional vibes way before they even met. 3 months goes by of them talking and texting every minute of the day. It was time to send it to her and April got her a ticket so now she's on her way. April shows her excitement smiling all day anxious like they were already together she said she want to see what she can do for her since she was in the army, and she just had supposedly got a 400,000 settlement. April then says she is doing big things and that she can do something with her and that she's not a bum b****, so maybe this will be the one. I'm like oh ok sure, so she's at the airport now and April goes and get her from the airport and of course she goes by herself which I had no problem with. They go out to eat of course, and then go live and show the world her new stud. It's a car meet today so me and son slide out and go make some videos for YouTube but when we got back it was like what for where's my wife? anyway you guessed it upstairs in that room with a new stud. All I heard was ha-ha and it was about 9pm. I go to my/our room and chill and watch some tv next thing you know it's about 12am and still not a peep from them no text no nothing so I'm like I guess I'll go to sleep and see what tomorrow brings. I woke up alone with nobody in my bed, I laughed in my head lol, so I shower go live it's about 2pm now and still haven't seen April. I'm live we talking, and they asked me how's the new girlfriend? And what do you think of her? Have you met Bentley? I say no I haven't, they still sleep then 2 minutes later April opens the door and say you want to meet her? I'm like I guess so fasho she has to force her to come to the door and say wassup with a stank face and walk off. I'm like wassup oh ok cool nice to meet you, I never said nothing else to the girl but she had some things to say about me already and I didn't like it cause I didn't know why all of the hatred was towards me cause I haven't said nothing to the girl but I guess she had her reasons cause of whatever April had told her about me and texted her over those months but its whatever. I go on about my day as they do theirs and leave for the day and go out to eat, me and her daughter went to look for cars at a car lot for the new baby, but we had no luck that day. While we were out, April and her new girl was on live, and I can hear her talking smack about me then she gets on by herself and tells the people to take me off their hands somebody please take the ninja off our hands so we can be happy but then April says nothing about it. I said wow, also a couple of other things were said as well, yall seen it and if yall didn't go look on Facebook, TikTok, YouTube you'll see everything. I'm saying to be facts type in Ivan Edwards or The Edwards Empire and everything should pop up, so I just acted like I didn't see it, but all my followers made sure I seen everything so I'm just thinking in my head why haven't April checked her? And why did she stay quiet and tucked her tail? That's when I saw her queen crown fall off her head, but I kept cool. The next day I woke up to some food sitting on my dresser at 7am which I told yall we don't eat that early because she didn't want to get up until 2/4pm so all of sudden you want to make breakfast in bed for your new stud and bring me the scrap plate breakfast and sit it on the dresser and not even wake me up. They are in the kitchen being loud as a football game in there so of course I wake up and text her just to tell her to quiet down so I can go to sleep please. They ended up going upstairs so I fell back asleep. 3 hours later I woke back up I go live I wake n bake with my people, they asked me if I got some breakfast, I said oh yeah, it's cold now I threw it away. That's when all hell broke loose the internet can be messy sometimes, they went back and told April and then her stud Bentley was upset and called me a b**** ass ninja on live while 1.9k people were watching and again April says nothing so now I'm highly upset with April. I texted her and told her that I don't think I'm going to be around if she continues to be here, I don't know if I can be here because you let her disrespect me and it's going to continue to happen, and I can't have that. She says "so when are you leaving? After I saw what she responded I said to myself that's crazy, and I didn't even respond back. Me and her daughter ended up going back to the car lot, they got blessed with the SUV they needed. When we got back to the house, I tried to walk in the garage to go and get my lil smoke and a shot of henny and while I was on my way in April stop me and say "what are you doing? I say huh? she says "what you doing? You said that you were done aint no coming back from that.

I say ok you want me to leave? She says I just don't want any problems with this girl. I say wow nobody thinking about her I just want to smoke and take a shot with the kids for their accomplishment because they just got a brand-new SUV which she never even looked at, she didn't even say congratulations or anything she was just trying to push me out. I go in the room get my jar and my bottle and sit it down, next thing I know the new studdy downstairs mumbling stuff under her breath, April's daughter asked her why she even saying anything regarding me, so they argue then April she's hollering "the baby is right there so her daughter is really upset their neck to neck. April steps in and tells her daughter to leave get out and get that baby out of here, so she says of course you'd pick a b**** over your child and once again they argued. I told her just leave before yall get too crazy, ill grab my stuff and be over there later, so she gets in her car and starts it, but her wife is messy she stands outside hoping someone's say something to her. I'm grabbing my stuff putting it in my car trying to leave peacefully but stud girl still trying to argue yelling and telling April's daughter wife saying "I'll take a shot with you after your wife gets out of the car and apologizes to me as if she was somebody. I grabbed the shot glass and threw it on the floor, and I told them to leave please before it got crazy. I go back to walk in the door Bentley puts her arm up and blocks me from walking in I say excuse me and she says no because I was talking to her and you told her to leave so now, I'm talking to you. I said watch out and popped her arm off me with my chest and walked through the door then she started calling me names and bucking up at me. What does April do grab her and tell me to leave because she's a female, I buck back up of course I'm not gone hit her/him but I'm not going to show fear either. Then April said where was that energy for the other studdy? But with her I didn't have to do that; she has known me all of them years, it's only been 2 days and I don't know this if you feel me. I should've smacked her just because lol but that's not me. I might have been that ninja that day. Luckily son came and grabbed me and told me he would just bring all my stuff over there just go ahead and go so I said OK I'm gone, and I started crying. April says you don't love me, or you wouldn't be leaving! I said if you loved me, you would send this demon back to where she came from! She then said no you could leave, so I started crying, tears just flowing for real, and I haven't cried in so long. I had to pull over at the gas station until I stopped crying and was able to drive. When I got to their house I went live and cry some more and afterwards I went to sleep. In the morning, I go back live telling my side of the story and all of a sudden, my live gets cut off, I started it back over and it gets cut off again so it can only be April, so I make a post and say I need a new page she deletes my post. I'm like come on now then 2 seconds later she walks up, I'm in the backyard she says if I stop poly would you come back? I said no! she said if I gave up women completely would you come back? I said no! She said there's nothing I can do. I said, "is the girl still at the house? she said yes, I said well that's who you want cause it wouldn't have been me if I had a lady who was only there for me and tripped on my wife I would've told the girl to pack her stuff back up and get tf out she's not going to disrespect my wife like that sorry not sorry but that's just me. She thinks about what I just said and then gone say "are you sure this is what you want to do? I say I gotta let you spread your wings and fly and be happy. She says ok and makes herself cry and walks off. I didn't even look, I just kept my head straight because I didn't want to look at her and change my mind, it's time to live for me. I ended up going to the office where the girls stayed and applied for my own apartment, and they said that I can move in on the 16th of May. It was some people who came looking around being nosey so I went back into the office, and I asked for an emergency move in if it was possible so she said that she'll call me back if it can happen. The lady in the office called me back and said that if my credit was good and if I had the money, then I could move in on the first, which was the next day. I had the money, so I moved in my first apartment, my first time alone, my first time doing my own thing, it's going to be crazy but ill handle it, God got me.

Chapter 28

New Life

Trying to find myself in a bottle and strippers we were invited to this event but now it's just me, I still want to go I don't like to be a no show I will pop up wherever I'm invited so yes invite me out hit me up you know the vibes. I ended up going to this event just to have a good time. I was chillin throwing dollars for a little bit then I left. The next day I went to a buddy house to chill, I ended up seeing one of the ladies from the past and she looked like she was expecting me as if it was a setup? Right! She was fresh out of the shower and stuff so whatever we smoked then afterwards I was about to dip back to my place before my furniture had got delivered. She wants to come I'm like I don't know but why not who do I have at home nobody so why not let's go. She grabbed her bag, and we slid out. We chillin at the house, we smoked, we did some random things. We have been hanging out for a week on and off.

I started to tell the girl in my car club about the situation by me leaving and getting my own place. I was about to go home and she said can she come with me and I said why not we got a room already before after I left the house so yea you can come to my house, so instead of paying for a room she came over a couple of times then I get a call out of nowhere this lady say she wants to meet me and hang out and stuff I say sure why not so she came from Dallas and we chilled and that was that. I needed my hair done so I made a post and said who can do my hair? I got a message saying I can do your hair; I don't know if you remember me, but we talked once before on snap. I say not really but yea she said you can come to my house, or I can go to yours, I know you like to smoke, and I have children, I said OK cool come through. She came through and she's nervously doing my hair. We smoked and that's it not too many words at all then the next day or two I get a message saying you should let me come cook for you in my lingerie for Father's Day her knowing Father's Day was two weeks away, so I say sure come over she does cook and feed my mind, body and soul. She comes back the next day and this time I don't want to eat food, I want to eat something else, and it was good and had a great smell, so you know I licked the plate clean. The next day I chilled with the girl from the car club in the daytime and then the girl from the strip club at nighttime.

The next day after that I chilled with girl from Dallas, she tells me that she's pregnant, whhhaaattttt? She shows me the test I'm like nah no way my s*** don't even work, I don't think I can have any kids. She goes back to Dallas. Basically, I've been wilding out, but I didn't even care, I've been locked tf up basically in a cell with a guard who gave me 20 minutes in the yard then back in a cell but yall get it, so yea. I cut up for a minute now its Father's Day and I'm chilling 6pm comes I leave to go outside and hang with the guys and as soon as I pull up and get out of my car the cops pull in the lot right behind me and tells me to get back in the car and roll my window down. I did what I was told so he walked up, opened my door and grabbed me and put me in handcuffs. He asked me why I was driving like that, and I said something like what? He said that I made a donut and a burnout, I said you got the wrong guy! He said OK and put me in the back of the police car. Everyone that's standing around is calling him names and asking him why I in the car am he then say nothing, he walks back to the car after searching my hellcat for drugs, I guess. I told the officer that I have a firearm, he said where? I say in the backseat of the passenger pocket door. He couldn't see it, he had to move my seat to get it out of the pocket, he walked back with it cocked open and sits it on the seat and close the door. 20 minutes later a tow truck comes, I'm thinking like why he's even towing my car, he walks back up. I say can you tell me something he say you're going to jail; I say why? He said UCW bro I say what's that? He says unlawful carry of weapon. I say how and I wasn't even carrying it? He said you had it in plain sight. I said how and you had to look for it? He says you have to have it in a holster. I say well damn that sounds like a warning to me, like you can let me go. He says I can't the DA already picked up the charge, now he was lying they didn't even answer the phone. I'm watching him call over and over, so now they tow my car away and he took me around the corner and searched my car again for drugs. He cut my seat and carpet looking for stuff with his stupid ass he never looked where the blunts was. I had a lil bleezy rolled up and tucked somewhere but he was looking for drugs and because of my jewelry I believed he profiled me and assumed that I was a dealer or something. I said can you get all my stuff out of the car? He does and then he takes me to jail, it was my first time at 30 years old went to jail for nothing. I was so upset but I'm like its whatever, I guess there wasn't anything that I could do. We made down to the station; he puts me in the system and says oh you have an LTC? I said yes oh that's a license to carry a handgun, he says oh ok and continues to book me and then he asked me if I was in a gang I said no. They took my cash, put it on a card and they put my jewelry in a bag. I'm really in jail thinking I didn't even do anything lol wtf, so I go to the back its 60 mfs in here all races all sizes or whatever. They said that I can use the phone so I'm on the phone making my calls like who can come and get me, and no I did not call April at all get that out your head. I called the girl from the car club; she says oh I just pulled up when they were taking you. I wanted to tell you something, I said what you're pregnant? She says yes, I am, she then says and that's not what I was going to tell you but yea I am. I say is it mine? she says yes, you're the only one that I've been with. I say ok cool I'm excited, she says but I can't stay on the phone call come and see me when you get out, I'm like cool click.

Chapter 29

False Identity

I call my stylist you know we cool and s***, so I'm like whoop whoop she like hit me when you get out so I'm like damn nobody got me. I hit the home girl up, she stayed on the phone and chopped it up. I then called my stylist back she like your bond is 100 dollars imma come and get you I'm like cool, then I call back in like 5 minutes to see what they said she said that there was no bond and that there holding me. I say why? she says it's multiple felonies on your name. I say whaaaaattt! who me there's no way, so now I can't get bailed out they called me to a window hours later and asked me for my social and tells me that I'm a felon from Maryland named Isaiah Edwards 6,2 born in 1991. I said oh yea yall need to fix this, because my name is Ivan Edwards from Los Angeles 5,7 born in 1992 so yea yall messed up. He says well if they don't fix it, you'll be called to another window soon. I don't know what to tell you. I started seeing everyone leaving getting bailed out and I'm like when can I go, so I go this other window talking to the lady and I asked her about what they were telling me, she made a call and tells me go back out there she gone come back out and if I see her then walk back up to her. It's been 4 hours and here she comes she told me that she fixed everything and that I will be fine, and I will get a free bond she then told me to just wait 4 more hours until the courts open, I say ok. I go to court; the judge admits their mistake on the felony part and tells me that I can leave in the next couple of minutes, which turned into a couple of more hours, but I still was able to use the phone. I called and told my stylist that I was about to get out and she said "I'm outside with 2 rolled up, I said shut tf up are you for real. When they opened that door, she was right there, I hopped in and got tf on. I went and got my car but went right back there the next Sunday. I got pulled over again and that's when I said it got to be this hellcat. I sold it and went and got me a Camaro. Now I'm taking a trip to Cali, I was scared and got tf on. I messed around and stayed out there like a week, my stylist had dropped me off and picked me up from the airport. I got back and got a message a lil while later saying I'm pregnant. I'm like another one fuck it lets go we finally getting somewhere in life, I'm about to have a litter all it took was for me to leave the one I been trying with all my life and that's crazy. I think she was pushing the stuff out so we couldn't have one well I know back in the day she did but was still doing it after we were married so I think she never wanted a baby with me which was fine. Look at how things ended up going for me, now that I'm out of jail, I am ready to get tf on and go tell my family what happened, so I asked my stylist to come through and hook me up and she offers to take me to the airport and pick me up when I get back. I get out there, I fool around with some people who never got a chance to even talk to me but were in the same relationship you know just to see what's up. I chilled with some family for a while it happened to be the 4th of July and stripper girl just so happens to pop up talking about, I'm in La can you smoke with me, I'm like sure why not. We went to the hood and then we chilled we watched the fireworks and all. We chilled until I was ready to go. When I got back it seemed like all the ladies wanted to come over, so I let them know that I was back at home, but I'd rather just chill with stylist I told her bout ol girl being pregnant she laughed and said now you got 2 gfs and one baby momma. I laughed and thought nothing of it. She said it again a couple days later and I said who? she told me and the girl from the club. I laughed and said that I don't want no girlfriend and that I wanna be a whore lol. That didn't last too long between these 2 and my new baby momma, I didn't have time to do too much, one was under me like rice under gravy but annoying though because she didn't know how to be in a real relationship, she was a whore for real, but I didn't know at the time. I thought she just threw butt in a circle or square but whatever so the 2 was talking about coming over at the same time I said that's on yall but I don't want no BS at my spot. They ended up coming around the same time, we kicked it, and everything were going smooth, I tell them I'm going to Mississippi for my first family reunion then my stylist says we are going too, I say that's cool yall can ride together my stylist then say that's cool and that she can have somebody to keep her company. So cool that's the plan, I told them that I can mess with both of y'all if they want and try Poly since they know about it already. We gave it a shot and we went to sleep. That night the girl from the club got upset and was angry because she didn't get held all night, so she got up and slept in the living room just being weird. When it was time to go in the morning, we were leaving out the door and while we were walking, she stayed behind us making videos of us leaving her behind, but she stayed behind us on purpose just to make the video so make it make sense. She just started being weird really fast so y'all know she's going to the family reunion, and

I told her I was going by myself to avoid hearing her mouth since she was already going crazy. She seen on snap that I was in the passenger seat heading to Mississippi, she called me and cursed me out but she was just in California with me on the 4th of July so she should have just relaxed and waited for us to get back but no she was acting really crazy or whatever. We get to the family reunion, and they treated her with so much love and she was so respectful, we had such a great time and being that it was my first family reunion my family never seen my wife, so they just assumed she was my wife, so I had to say she's, my girlfriend. They didn't care, they were just happy to see us period. My mother and sister welcomed her with open arms, we chillewd and went everywhere together, I said "I might have a gf now in my head lol so now it's time to head back home a whole 7-hour drive. Soon as we got back the girl was at my door knocking on it like the police. I looked to see a baby, so I open it they rush in trying to talk like everything is cool, but we had to make a trip, so we let them hang for a little bit, but she thought she was going to be able to stay, nah she had to go with the rest of them so she was upset and sad. I didn't understand the part she played but it was over for her, but she wasn't done she started talking crazy on the internet and ended up going to April house and making videos talking about me and trying to make me look bad and saying false things on my name the both of them had me messed up for real. I thought April would keep my name out of her mouth, but she couldn't. I got a knock on the door and it's the police. I farted, he handed me these papers and said good luck. I got the divorce papers oh it's real now, so I went to court I signed the papers and a month later I was divorced and free from all the stress. Not so much drama even though April would not leave me or my girlfriend alone on the internet, her and the girl from the strip club kept talking s*** and they still are until this day. I just said I'm not going to respond I'm going to write a book, and this is what I'm doing oh but we off them now. NEXT

Chapter 30

What Baby?

Where's the baby? You said it and I said the same thing. That's why I said earlier April glammed me, so the girl comes back in town comes to Sunday fun day walks right past me and talks to all the guys. She's been gone a whole month or 2, I haven't talked to her since that night that I was in jail so I'm thinking she got some words for me but no she walked right past me and said nothing. I hit her up after she was brief but said she will call me back, so I waited. Another week goes by and we back at Sunday fun day, she walks right past me again. After that night this time my girlfriend hit her up like wassup what yall doing, and they talked for an hour. My girl says "I didn't check on the baby, I only asked her how she was doing. I say whhatttt so I called her, she says "I'll call you back. Once again, I say ok then another week goes by, I see her back outside, that's when I asked her for an ultrasound or something like I don't even know if she really pregnant or not. She says I need to talk to you, I already knew what that meant so I said tell me then she said no because you're a social media person you're going to tell my business I said just tell me, she says she doesn't want to be a single parent and she just can't do it so I said do I have a say? so she said NO! and that she's going to Mexico to get it done. Oh well I guess its still not meant to be maybe it won't ever who knows and who cares. I see her every Sunday. She stares at me and keeps pushing, I will never talk to her or April or the stripper ever again I wouldn't care if they're on fire I wouldn't even spit on them. Yall seen how they did me so now it's just my girlfriend and I and we are trying to live our life with the kids but everyone on the internet is mad and hating because I said I would not get a girlfriend, but it just happened. I wanted to be happy, single and living young wild and free but the closer we got the happier I became with life and to finally see someone who asks if I'm ok? who checks on my well-being, who actually misses me after they leave, who accepts me for me even with all the drama she has to endure day by day. The stress I cause just being a man and a somewhat celebrity to the world, so you know it's kind of hard. She feels that she has to uphold a certain lifestyle but it aint nothing to cut some s*** off. I am no longer Poly I only want one woman and to have a little fun every now and then but that's only if she's up for it but that was only once which I'm fine with that even if it never happens again, I'm still cool with just her. We both are happy, and we will continue to do our thing, if God Is willing, He will make a way for us according to His riches and Glory. The Lord adds blessings to the readers of this book and let it be a lesson to never let nobody and I repeat nobody have control over your life. Do what you want and not what the world wants you to do, remember that having peace is free and yall know we broke so I'll take it.

Thank you and God Bless.

End The Live, Delete or Save.

Declaration

I Ivan Edwards declare that the stories in this book are true. These stories are not meant to hurt anybody's character or reputation. This book has been written to share my truths and life experiences. This book is not meant to hurt anyone. The purpose of this book is to prevent an avenue of escape for those who may have encountered the shortcomings mentioned in this book. The names have been changed in this book to protect me and the people characterized in this book yall know who yall are and yall know who they are. May God get the Glory for all souls that get saved because of this book Amen.

www.ingramcontent.com/pod-product-compliance
Lightning Source LLC
Chambersburg PA
CBHW072130160426
43197CB00012B/2053